D0103635

The Power of a Praying™ Wife
Prayer Cards

Stormie Omartian

HARVEST HOUSE PUBLISHERS
Eugene, Oregon 97402

All Scripture verses are taken from the New King James Version,
Copyright © 1979, 1980, 1982 by Thomas Nelson, Inc., Publishers.
Used by permission.

Cover by Koechel Peterson & Associates, Minneapolis, Minnesota

POWER OF A PRAYING WIFE PRAYER CARDS

Copyright © 2000 by Stormie Omartian
Published by Harvest House Publishers
Eugene, Oregon 97402

ISBN 0-7369-0471-9

Printed in Hong Kong

01 02 03 04 05 06 07 / NG-CF / 10 9 8 7 6 5 4 3

Introduction

When I wrote the book *The Power of a Praying Wife*, I received countless letters filled with testimonies of restored marriages and changed lives. I was deeply touched by the hearts of women who were willing to do anything to see their marriages become all God wanted them to be. Included in many of the letters were requests to have the prayers in this book made available separately so they could be carried in a purse, taped to a refrigerator door, put on a desk at work, or placed in some convenient location as a reminder of how to pray that day. Some women told me they had even resorted to tearing a particular prayer out of the book in order to carry it around with them. That fervency and those requests are what led me to the idea of these prayer cards.

In the midst of our busy lives, it's often hard to know how to pray beyond the immediate or urgent. That's why praying from these prayer cards will set your mind at peace, knowing that when you have prayed each prayer, you will have covered your husband and your marriage thoroughly. Not only will *he* be blessed, but the rewards will be great for *you,* too. There are blessings that will come to you from God simply because you are praying.

Don't be overwhelmed by the many ways there are to pray for your husband. You don't have to do it all in one day, one week, or even one month. Just pick a card, any card, and let the Holy Spirit lead you from there. And don't worry about the answers. As long as you look to God as the source of all you want to see happen in your husband and your marriage, you don't have to be concerned about how it will happen. It's *your* job to *pray.* It's *God's* job to *answer.* Leave it in His hands.

—*Stormie Omartian*

His Wife

*L*ord, help me to be a good wife. I fully realize that I don't have what it takes to be one without Your help. Take my selfishness, impatience, and irritability and turn them into kindness, long-suffering, and the willingness to bear all things. Take my old emotional habits, mindsets, automatic reactions, rude assumptions, and self-protectiveness, and make me patient, kind, good, faithful, gentle, and self-controlled. Take the hardness of my heart and break down the walls with Your battering ram of revelation. Give me a new heart and work in me Your love, peace, and joy (Galatians 5:22,23). I am not able to rise above who I am at this moment. Only You can transform me.

*W*hatever things you ask when you pray, believe that you receive them,
and you will have them. And whenever you stand praying,
if you have anything against anyone, forgive him,
that your Father in heaven may also forgive your trespasses.

Mark 11:24, 25

Chapter 1a

His Wife

Lord, I confess the times I've been unloving, critical, angry, resentful, disrespectful, or unforgiving toward my husband. Help me to put aside any hurt, anger, or disappointment I feel and forgive him the way You do—totally and completely, no looking back. Make me a tool of reconciliation, peace, and healing in this marriage. Make me my husband's helpmate, companion, champion, friend, and support. Help me to create a peaceful, restful, safe place for him to come home to. Teach me how to take care of myself and stay attractive to him. Grow me into a creative and confident woman who is rich in mind, soul, and spirit. Make me the kind of woman he can be proud to say is his wife.

❧❧❧

Through wisdom a house is built, and by understanding it is established; by knowledge the rooms are filled with all precious and pleasant riches.

PROVERBS 24:3,4

His Wife

$\mathcal{L}$ord, I lay all my expectations at Your cross. I release my husband from the burden of fulfilling me in areas where I should be looking to You. Help me to accept him the way he is and not try to change him. I realize that in some ways he may never change, but at the same time, I release him to change in ways I never thought he could. I leave any changing that needs to be done in Your hands, fully accepting that neither of us is perfect and never will be. Only You, Lord, are perfect, and I look to You to perfect us. May we be "perfectly joined together in the same mind and in the same judgment" (1 Corinthians 1:10).

❧❧❧

$\mathcal{B}$e kind to one another, tenderhearted, forgiving one another, even as God in Christ forgave you.

EPHESIANS 4:32

His Wife

*L*ord, teach me how to pray for my husband and make my prayers a true language of love. Where love has died, create new love between us. Show me what unconditional love really is and how to communicate it in a way he can clearly perceive. Bring unity between us so that we can be in agreement about everything (Amos 3:3). May the God of patience and comfort grant us to be like-minded toward one another, according to Christ Jesus (Romans 15:5). Make us a team, not pursuing separate, competitive, or independent lives, but working together, overlooking each other's faults and weaknesses for the greater good of the marriage. Help us to pursue the things which make for peace and the things by which one may edify another (Romans 14:19).

❧❧❧

*L*et us not grow weary while doing good,
for in due season we shall reap if we do not lose heart.

GALATIANS 6:9

His Wife

*L*ord, I pray that the commitment my husband and I have to You and to one another will grow stronger and more passionate every day. Enable him to be the head of the home as You made him to be, and show me how to support and respect him as he rises to that place of leadership. Reveal to me what he wants and needs and show me potential problems before they arise. Breathe Your life into this marriage. Make me a new person, Lord. Give me a fresh perspective, a positive outlook, and a renewed relationship with the man You've given me. Help me see him with new eyes, new appreciation, new love, new compassion, and new acceptance. Give my husband a new wife, and let it be me.

❧❧

*A*sk, and it will be given to you; seek, and you will find; knock, and it will be opened to you. For everyone who asks receives, and he who seeks finds, and to him who knocks it will be opened.

MATTHEW 7:7,8

His Work

*L*ord, I pray that You would bless the work of my husband's hands. May his labor bring not only favor, success, and prosperity, but great fulfillment as well. If the work he is doing is not in line with Your perfect will for his life, reveal it to him. Show him what he should do differently and guide him down the right path. Give him strength, faith, and a vision for the future so he can rise above any propensity for laziness. May he never run from work out of fear, selfishness, or a desire to avoid responsibility. On the other hand, help him to see that he doesn't have to work himself to death for man's approval. Give him the ability to enjoy his success without striving for more. Help him to excel, but free him from the pressure to do so.

❧❧❧

Do you see a man who excels in his work? He will stand before kings; he will not stand before unknown men.

PROVERBS 22:29

His Work

*G*od, I pray that You will be Lord over my husband's work. May he bring You into every aspect of it. Give him enough confidence in the gifts You've placed in him to be able to seek, find, and do good work. Open up doors of opportunity for him that no man can close. Develop his skills so that they grow more valuable with each passing year. Show me what I can do to encourage him. I pray that his work will be established, secure, successful, satisfying, and financially rewarding. Let him be like a tree planted by the stream of Your living water, which brings forth fruit in due season. May he never wither under pressure, but grow strong and prosper (Psalm 1:3).

❧❧❧

*Let the beauty of the L*ORD *our God be upon us,*
and establish the work of our hands for us;
yes, establish the work of our hands.

PSALM 90:17

His Finances

*L*ord, I commit our finances to You. Be in charge of them and use them for Your purposes. May my husband and I be good stewards of all that You give us and walk in total agreement as to how it is to be disbursed. I pray that we will learn to live free of burdensome debt. Where we have not been wise, bring restoration and give us guidance. Show me how I can help increase our finances and not decrease them unwisely. Help us to remember that all we have belongs to You and to be grateful for it.

❧❧❧

*D*o not seek what you should eat or what
you should drink, nor have an anxious mind.
For all these things the nations of the world seek after,
and your Father knows that you need these things.
But seek the kingdom of God,
and all these things shall be added to you.

Luke 12:29-31

His Finances

Lord, I pray that (husband's name) will have wisdom to handle money wisely. Help him make good decisions as to how he spends. Show him how to plan for the future. Teach him to give as You have instructed in Your Word. I pray that he will find the perfect balance between spending needlessly and being miserly. May he always be paid well for the work he does, and may his money not be stolen, lost, devoured, destroyed, or wasted. Multiply it so that what he makes will go a long way. I pray that he will not be anxious about finances, but will seek Your kingdom first, knowing that as he does, we will have all we need (Luke 12:31).

❧❧❧

My God shall supply all your need
according to His riches in glory by Christ Jesus.

PHILIPPIANS 4:19

His Sexuality

*L*ord, bless my husband's sexuality and make it an area of great fulfillment for him. Restore what needs to be restored, balance what needs to be balanced. Protect us from apathy, disappointment, criticism, busyness, unforgiveness, deadness, or disinterest. I pray that we make time for one another, communicate our true feelings openly, and remain sensitive to what each other needs. Keep us sexually pure in mind and body, and close the door to anything lustful or illicit that seeks to encroach upon us. Deliver us from the bondage of past mistakes. Remove completely the effects of any sexual experience—in thought or deed—that has ever happened to us outside of our relationship. Purify us by the power of Your Spirit.

❧❧❧

*F*lee sexual immorality. Every sin that a man does is outside the body, but he who commits sexual immorality sins against his own body. Or do you not know that your body is the temple of the Holy Spirit who is in you, whom you have from God, and you are not your own? For you were bought at a price; therefore glorify God in your body and in your spirit, which are God's.

1 CORINTHIANS 6:18-20

His Sexuality

*L*ord, take away anyone or anything from my husband's life that would inspire temptation to infidelity. Help him to "abstain from sexual immorality" so that he will know "how to possess his own vessel in sanctification and honor" (1 Thessalonians 4:3,4). I pray that we will desire each other and no one else. Show me how to make myself attractive and desirable to him and be the kind of partner he needs. I pray that neither of us will ever be tempted to think about seeking fulfillment elsewhere. I realize that an important part of my ministry to my husband is sexual. Help me to never use it as a weapon or a means of manipulation by giving and withholding it for selfish reasons. I commit this area of our lives to You, Lord. May it be continually new and alive. Make it all that You created it to be.

❧❧

The body is not for sexual immorality
but for the Lord, and the Lord for the body.

1 CORINTHIANS 6:13

His Affection

$\mathcal{L}$ord, I pray for open physical affection between my husband and me. Enable each of us to lay aside self-consciousness or apathy and be effusive in our display of love. Help us to demonstrate how much we care for and value each other. Remind us throughout each day to affectionately touch one another in some way. Help us to not be cold, undemonstrative, uninterested, or remote. Enable us to be warm, tender, compassionate, loving, and adoring. Break through any hardheaded-ness on our part that refuses to change and grow. If one of us is less affectionate to the other's detriment, bring us into balance. Change our habits of indifference so that we can become the husband and wife You called us to be.

❧❦

So husbands ought to love their own wives as their own bodies; he who loves his wife loves himself. For no one ever hated his own flesh, but nourishes and cherishes it, just as the Lord does the church.

EPHESIANS 5:28,29

His Temptations

*L*ord, I pray that You would strengthen my husband to resist any temptation that comes his way. Deliver him from evils such as adultery, pornography, drugs, alcohol, gambling, and perversion. Remove temptation especially in the area of (name of specific temptation). Make him strong where he is weak. Help him to rise above anything that seeks to erect a stronghold in his life. Lord, You've said that "whoever has no rule over his own spirit is like a city broken down, without walls" (Proverbs 25:28). I pray that (husband's name) will not be broken down by the power of evil, but raised up by the power of God. Help him to take charge over his own spirit and have self-control to resist anything and anyone who becomes a temptation.

❧❧❧

No temptation has overtaken you except such as is common to man; but God is faithful, who will not allow you to be tempted beyond what you are able, but with the temptation will also make the way of escape, that you may be able to bear it.

1 CORINTHIANS 10:13

His Mind

Lord, I pray for Your protection on my husband's mind. Shield him from the lies of the enemy. Help him to clearly discern between Your voice and any other, and show him how to take every thought captive as You have instructed us to do. May he thirst for Your Word and hunger for Your truth so that he can recognize wrong thinking. Give him strength to resist lying thoughts. Where the enemy's lies have already invaded his thoughts, cleanse his mind. Lord, You have given me authority "over all the power of the enemy" (Luke 10:19). By that authority given to me in Jesus Christ, I command all lying spirits away from my husband's mind. I proclaim that You, God, have given (husband's name) a sound mind.

❧❧❧

Though we walk in the flesh, we do not war according to the flesh.
For the weapons of our warfare are not carnal but mighty in God
for pulling down strongholds, casting down arguments and every high thing
that exalts itself against the knowledge of God, bringing every thought
into captivity to the obedience of Christ.

2 CORINTHIANS 10:3-5

His Mind

*L*ord, I pray that my husband will not entertain confusion in his mind, but will live in clarity. Keep him from being tormented with impure, evil, negative, or sinful thoughts. Enable him to be transformed by the renewing of his mind (Romans 12:2). Help him to be anxious for nothing, but in everything by prayer and supplication, with thanksgiving, let his requests be made known to You; and may Your peace, which surpasses all understanding, guard his heart and mind through Christ Jesus (Philippians 4:6,7). And finally, whatever things are true, noble, just, pure, lovely, of good report, having virtue, or anything praiseworthy, let him think on these things (Philippians 4:8).

❧❧❧

To be carnally minded is death,
but to be spiritually minded is life and peace.

ROMANS 8:6

His Fears

*L*ord, You've said in Your Word that "there is no fear in love; but perfect love casts out fear, because fear involves torment. But he who fears has not been made perfect in love" (1 John 4:18). I pray You will perfect my husband in Your love so that tormenting fear finds no place in him. I know You have not given him a spirit of fear. You've given him power, love, and a sound mind (2 Timothy 1:7). I pray in the name of Jesus that fear will not rule over my husband. Instead, may Your Word penetrate every fiber of his being, convincing him that Your love for him is far greater than anything he faces and nothing can separate him from it.

❧✦❧

The angel of the Lord *encamps all around those who fear Him, and delivers them.*

Psalm 34:7

His Fears

Lord, I pray that my husband will acknowledge You as a Father whose love is unfailing, whose strength is without equal, and in whose presence there is nothing to fear. Deliver him this day from fear that destroys and replace it with godly fear (Jeremiah 32:40). Teach him Your way, O Lord. Help him to walk in Your truth. Unite his heart to fear Your name (Psalm 86:11). May he have no fear of men, but rise up and boldly say, "The LORD is my helper; I will not fear. What can man do to me?" (Hebrews 13:6). "How great is Your goodness, which You have laid up for those who fear You" (Psalm 31:19).

❧❧❧

Fear not, for I am with you; be not dismayed,
for I am your God. I will strengthen you, yes,
I will help you, I will uphold you
with My righteous right hand.

ISAIAH 41:10

His Fears

I say to you, (husband's name), "Be strong, do not fear! Behold, your God will come with vengeance, with the recompense of God; He will come and save you" (Isaiah 35:4). "In righteousness you shall be established; you shall be far from oppression, for you shall not fear" (Isaiah 54:14). "You shall not be afraid of the terror by night, nor of the arrow that flies by day, nor of the pestilence that walks in darkness, nor of the destruction that lays waste at noonday" (Psalm 91:5,6). May the Spirit of the Lord rest upon you, "the Spirit of wisdom and understanding, the Spirit of counsel and might, the Spirit of knowledge and of the fear of the LORD" (Isaiah 11:2).

❧❧

I sought the LORD, and He heard me,
and delivered me from all my fears.

PSALM 34:4

His Purpose

*L*ord, I pray that (husband's name) will clearly hear the call You have on his life. Help him to realize who he is in Christ and give him certainty he was created for a high purpose. Enable him to walk worthy of his calling and remind him of what You've called him to be. Don't let him get sidetracked with things that are unessential to Your purpose. Strike down discouragement so that it will not defeat him. Lift his eyes above the circumstances of the moment so he can see the purpose for which You created him. Give him patience to wait for Your perfect timing. I pray that the desires of his heart will not be in conflict with the desires of Yours. May he seek You for direction and hear when You speak to his soul.

❧❦❧

The God of our Lord Jesus Christ, the Father of glory…give to you the spirit of wisdom and revelation in the knowledge of Him, the eyes of your understanding being enlightened; that you may know what is the hope of His calling, what are the riches of the glory of His inheritance in the saints.

EPHESIANS 1:17,18

His Choices

*L*ord, fill my husband with the fear of the Lord and give him wisdom for every decision he makes. May he reverence You and Your ways and seek to know Your truth. Give him discernment to make decisions based on Your revelation. Help him to make godly choices and keep him from doing anything foolish. I pray that he will listen to godly counselors and not be a man who is unteachable. Instruct him even as he is sleeping (Psalm 16:7), and in the morning, I pray he will do what's right rather than follow the leading of his own flesh. May he not buy into the foolishness of this world, but keep his eyes on You and have ears to hear Your voice.

A wise man will hear and increase learning,
and a man of understanding will attain wise counsel.

<small>PROVERBS 1:5</small>

His Health

*L*ord, I pray for Your healing touch on (husband's name). Make every part of his body function the way You designed it to. Wherever there is anything out of balance, set it in perfect working order. Heal him of any disease, illness, injury, infirmity, or weakness. Strengthen his body to successfully endure his workload, and when he sleeps may he wake up completely rested, rejuvenated, and refreshed. I pray that he will have the desire to take care of his body, to eat the kind of food that brings health, to get regular exercise, and avoid anything that would be harmful to him. Help him to understand that his body is Your temple and he should care for it as such (1 Corinthians 3:16).

❧❧❧

I have heard your prayer,
I have seen your tears;
surely I will heal you.

2 KINGS 20:5

His Health

*L*ord, I pray that You will give my husband a strong heart that doesn't fail. When he is ill, I pray You will sustain him and heal him. Fill him with Your joy to give him strength. Specifically, I pray for (mention any area of concern). Give him faith to say, "O Lord my God, I cried out to You, and You healed me" (Psalm 30:2). Thank You, Lord, that You are my Healer. I pray that my husband will live a long and healthy life and when death does come, may it be accompanied by peace and not unbearable suffering and agony. Thank You, Lord, that You will be there to welcome him into Your presence, and not a moment before Your appointed hour.

❦❧

They cried out to the Lord in their trouble,
and He saved them out of their distresses.
He sent His word and healed them,
and delivered them from their destructions.

Psalm 107:19,20

His Protection

*L*ord, I pray that You would protect (husband's name) from any accidents, diseases, dangers, or evil influences. Keep him safe, especially in cars and planes. Hide him from violence and the plans of evil people. Wherever he walks, secure his steps. Keep him on Your path so that his feet don't slip (Psalm 17:5). If his foot does slip, hold him up by Your mercy (Psalm 94:18). Give him the wisdom and discretion that will help him walk safely and not fall into danger (Proverbs 3:21-23). Save him from any plans of the enemy that seek to destroy his life (Psalm 103:4). Preserve his going out and his coming in from this time forth and even forevermore (Psalm 121:8).

❧❧❧

He who dwells in the secret place of the Most High
shall abide under the shadow of the Almighty.
I will say of the LORD, "He is my refuge and my fortress;
my God, in Him I will trust."

PSALM 91:1,2

His Trials

Lord, You alone know the depth of the burden my husband carries. I may understand the specifics, but You have measured the weight of it on his shoulders. I've not come to minimize what You are doing in his life, for I know You work great things in the midst of trials. Nor am I trying to protect him from what he must face. I only want to support him so that he will get through this battle as the winner. Help him to remember that "the steps of a good man are ordered by the LORD, and He delights in his way. Though he fall, he shall not be utterly cast down; for the LORD upholds him with His hand" (Psalm 37:23,24).

❧❧

You have been grieved by various trials,
that the genuineness of your faith,
being much more precious than gold that perishes,
though it is tested by fire, may be found to praise,
honor, and glory at the revelation of Jesus Christ.

1 PETER 1:6,7

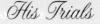

His Trials

*G*od, You are our refuge and strength, a very present help in trouble (Psalm 46:1). You have invited us to "come boldly to the throne of grace, that we may obtain mercy and find grace to help in time of need" (Hebrews 4:16). I come before Your throne and ask for grace for my husband. Strengthen his heart for this battle and give him patience to wait on You (Psalm 27:1-4). Build him up so that no matter what happens he will be able to stand strong through it. Help him to be always "rejoicing in hope, patient in tribulation, continuing steadfastly in prayer" (Romans 12:12). Give him endurance to run the race and not give up, for You have said that "a righteous man may fall seven times and rise again" (Proverbs 24:16).

You, who have shown me great and severe troubles, shall revive me again, and bring me up again from the depths of the earth. You shall increase my greatness, and comfort me on every side.

PSALM 71:20,21

His Trials

*L*ord, I pray that in the midst of trials my husband will look to You to be his refuge "until these calamities have passed by" (Psalm 57:1). May he learn to wait on You because "those who wait on the LORD shall renew their strength; they shall mount up with wings like eagles, they shall run and not be weary, they shall walk and not faint" (Isaiah 40:31). I pray that he will find his strength in You and as he cries out to You, You will hear him and save him out of all his troubles (Psalm 34:6). Teach him to cast his burdens on You and let You sustain him through everything that is happening in his life.

❧❧❧

*A*s for me, I will call upon God, and the LORD shall save me.
Evening and morning and at noon I will pray,
and cry aloud, and He shall hear my voice.
He has redeemed my soul in peace
from the battle that was against me.

PSALM 55:16-18

His Integrity

*L*ord, I pray that You would make my husband a man of integrity, according to Your standards. Give him strength to say "Yes" when he should say "Yes," and courage to say "No" when he should say "No." Enable him to stand for what he knows is right and not waver under pressure from the world. Don't let him be a man who is "always learning and never able to come to the knowledge of the truth" (2 Timothy 3:7). Give him, instead, a teachable spirit that is willing to listen to the voice of wisdom and grow in Your ways.

❧❧❧

The integrity of the upright will guide them,
but the perversity of the unfaithful will destroy them.

PROVERBS 11:3

His Integrity

Lord, I pray that You would make my husband a man who lives by truth. Help him to walk with Your Spirit of truth at all times (John 16:13). Be with him to bear witness to the truth so that in times of pressure he will act on it with confidence (1 John 1:8,9). Where he has erred in this and other matters, give him a heart that is quick to confess his mistakes. For You have said in Your Word, "If we say that we have no sin, we deceive ourselves, and the truth is not in us" (1 John 1:8). Don't let him be deceived. Don't let him live a lie in any way. Bind mercy and truth around his neck and write them on the tablet of his heart so he will find favor and high esteem in the sight of God and man (Proverbs 3:3,4).

❧❧❧

Better is the poor who walks in his integrity
than one perverse in his ways, though he be rich.

PROVERBS 28:6

His Reputation

Lord, I pray that (husband's name) will have a reputation that is untarnished. I know that a man is often valued "by what others say of him" (Proverbs 27:21), so I pray that he will be respected in our town and people will speak highly of him. You've said in Your Word that "a curse without cause shall not alight" (Proverbs 26:2). I pray that there would never be any reason for bad things to be said of him. Keep him out of legal entanglements. Protect us from lawsuits and criminal proceedings. Deliver him from his enemies, O God. Defend him from those who rise up to do him harm (Psalm 59:1). In You, O Lord, we put our trust. Let us never be put to shame (Psalm 71:1).

❧❧❧

Hide me from the secret plots of the wicked,
from the rebellion of the workers of iniquity,
who sharpen their tongue like a sword,
and bend their bows to shoot their arrows—bitter words.

PSALM 64:2,3

His Reputation

Lord, Your Word says that "a good tree cannot bear bad fruit, nor can a bad tree bear good fruit. Every tree that does not bear good fruit is cut down and thrown into the fire" (Matthew 7:18,19). I pray that my husband will bear good fruit out of the goodness that is within him, and that he will be known by the good that he does. May the fruits of honesty, trustworthiness, and humility sweeten all his dealings so that his reputation will never be spoiled. Preserve his life from the enemy, hide him from the secret counsel of the wicked. Pull him out of any net which has been laid for him (Psalm 31:4). If You are for us, who can be against us (Romans 8:31)?

❧❧❧

Do not let me be ashamed, O Lord, for I have called upon You;
let the wicked be ashamed; let them be silent in the grave.
Let the lying lips be put to silence, which speak insolent things
proudly and contemptuously against the righteous.

Psalm 31:17,18

His Reputation

*L*ord, I pray that You would keep my husband safe from the evil of gossiping mouths. Where there has been ill spoken of him, touch the lips of those who speak it with Your refining fire. Let them be ashamed and brought to confusion who seek to destroy his life; let them be driven backward and brought to dishonor who wish him evil (Psalm 40:14). May he trust in You and not be afraid of what man can do to him (Psalm 56:11). For You have said whoever believes in You will not be put to shame (Romans 10:11). Lead him, guide him, and be his mighty fortress and hiding place. May his light so shine before men that they see his good works and glorify You, Lord (Matthew 5:16).

❧❧❧

Blessed are you when they revile and persecute you,
and say all kinds of evil against you falsely for My sake.
Rejoice and be exceedingly glad, for great is your reward in heaven,
for so they persecuted the prophets who were before you.

MATTHEW 5:11,12

His Priorities

*L*ord, I pray for my husband's priorities to be in perfect order. Be Lord and Ruler over his heart. Help him to choose a simplicity of life that will allow him to have time alone with You, Lord, a place to be quiet in Your presence every day. Speak to him about making Your Word, prayer, and praise a priority. Enable him to place me and our children in greater prominence in his heart than career, friends, and activities. I pray he will seek You first and submit his all to You, for when he does I know the other pieces of his life will fit together perfectly. Help me to properly put my husband before children, work, family, friends, activities, and interests. Show me what I can do right now to demonstrate to him that he has this position in my heart.

❧✦❧

*S*eek first the kingdom of God and His righteousness,
and all these things shall be added to you.

MATTHEW 6:33

His Relationships

Lord, I pray for (husband's name) to have good, godly male friends with whom he can openly share his heart. May they be trustworthy men of wisdom who will speak truth into his life and not just say what he wants to hear (Proverbs 28:23). Give him the discernment to separate himself from anyone who will not be a good influence (1 Corinthians 5:13). Show him the importance of godly friendships and help me encourage him to sustain them. I pray for strong, peaceful relationships with each of his family members, neighbors, acquaintances, and coworkers. Today I specifically pray for his relationship with (name of person). Let there be reconciliation and peace where there has been estrangement.

❧❧❧

A new commandment I give to you, that you love one another; as I have loved you, that you also love one another. By this all will know that you are My disciples, if you have love for one another.

JOHN 13:34,35

His Relationships

Lord, I pray that You would enable my husband to be a forgiving person and not carry grudges or hold things in his heart against others. You've said in Your Word that "he who hates his brother is in darkness and walks in darkness, and does not know where he is going, because the darkness has blinded his eyes" (1 John 2:11). I pray that my husband would never be blinded by the darkness of unforgiveness, but continually walk in the light of forgiveness. Enable him to love his enemies, bless those who curse him, do good to those who hate him, and pray for those who spitefully use him and persecute him (Matthew 5:44). I pray that I will be counted as his best friend and our friendship will continue to grow.

❧❧❧

If you bring your gift to the altar, and there remember that your brother has something against you, leave your gift there before the altar, and go your way. First be reconciled to your brother, and then come and offer your gift.

MATTHEW 5:23,24

His Fatherhood

Lord, teach (husband's name) to be a good father. Where it was not modeled to him according to Your ways, heal those areas and help him to forgive his dad. Give him revelation of You and a hunger in his heart to really know You as his heavenly Father. Draw him close to spend time in Your presence so he can become more like You and fully understand Your Father's heart of compassion and love toward him. Grow that same heart in him for his children. Help him to balance mercy, judgment, and instruction the way You do. Though You require obedience, You are quick to acknowledge a repentant heart. Make him that way, too.

❧❧❧

Whom the LORD loves He corrects,
just as a father the son in whom he delights.
PROVERBS 3:12

His Fatherhood

*L*ord, I pray that my husband will understand how to discipline our children properly. May he never provoke his "children to wrath, but bring them up in the training and admonition of the Lord" (Ephesians 6:4). I pray we will be united in the rules we set for our children and be in full agreement as to how they are raised. I pray that there will be no strife or argument over how to handle them and the issues that surround their lives. Give him skills of communication with his children. I pray he will not be thought of by them as stern, hard, cruel, cold, and abusive, but rather may they see him as kind, softhearted, loving, warm, and affirming.

*C*hildren's children are the crown of old men,
and the glory of children is their father.

His Fatherhood

*L*ord, I pray that my husband will inspire his children to honor him as their father so that their lives will be long and blessed. May the spiritual inheritance he passes on to them be one rich in the fullness of Your Holy Spirit. Enable him to model clearly a walk of submission to Your laws. May he delight in his children and long to grow them up Your way. Help him not to be noncommunicative, passive, critical, weak, uninterested, neglectful, undependable, or uninvolved. Make him, instead, the kind of father who is interested, affectionate, involved, strong, consistent, dependable, verbally communicative, understanding, and patient. Being a good father is something he wants very much. I pray that You would give him that desire of his heart.

❧❧❧

The father of the righteous will greatly rejoice,
and he who begets a wise child will delight in him.

PROVERBS 23:24

His Past

*L*ord, I pray that You would enable (husband's name) to let go of his past completely. Deliver him from any hold it has on him. Help him to put off his former conduct and habitual ways of thinking about it and be renewed in his mind (Ephesians 4:22,23). Enlarge his understanding to know that You make all things new (Revelation 21:5). Show him a fresh, Holy Spirit-inspired way of relating to negative things that have happened. Give him the mind of Christ so that he can clearly discern Your voice from the voices of the past. When he hears those old voices, enable him to rise up and shut them down with the truth of Your Word.

❧❦❧

If anyone is in Christ, he is a new creation;
old things have passed away;
behold, all things have become new.

2 CORINTHIANS 5:17

His Past

*L*ord, I pray that wherever my husband has experienced rejection in his past, he would not allow that to color what he sees and hears now. Pour forgiveness into his heart so that bitterness, resentment, revenge, and unforgiveness will have no place there. May he regard the past as only a history lesson and not a guide for his daily life. Wherever his past has become an unpleasant memory, I pray You would redeem it and bring life out of it. Bind up his wounds (Psalm 147:3). Restore his soul (Psalm 23:3). Help him to release the past so that he will not live in it, but learn from it, break out of it, and move into the future You have for him.

❦

*D*o not remember the former things, nor consider the things of old.
Behold, I will do a new thing, now it shall spring forth;
shall you not know it? I will even make a road in
the wilderness and rivers in the desert.

ISAIAH 43:18,19

His Attitude

Lord, fill (husband's name) with Your love and peace today. May there be a calmness, serenity, and sense of well-being established in him because his life is God-controlled, rather than flesh-controlled. Enable him to walk in his house with a clean and perfect heart before You (Psalm 101:2). Shine the light of Your Spirit upon him and fill him with Your love. I pray that he will be kind and patient, not selfish or easily provoked. Release him from anger, unrest, anxiety, concerns, inner turmoil, strife, and pressure. Enable him to bear all things, believe all things, hope all things, and endure all things (1 Corinthians 13:7).

❧❧❧

Be anxious for nothing, but in everything by prayer and supplication,
with thanksgiving, let your requests be made known to God;
and the peace of God, which surpasses all understanding,
will guard your hearts and minds through Christ Jesus.

PHILIPPIANS 4:6,7

His Attitude

Lord, I pray that my husband will have a heart of thanksgiving. May he not be broken in spirit because of sorrow (Proverbs 15:13), but enjoy the continual feast of a merry heart (Proverbs 15:15). Give him a spirit of joy and keep him from growing into a grumpy old man. Help him to be anxious for nothing, but give thanks in all things so he can know the peace that passes all understanding. May he come to the point of saying, "I have learned in whatever state I am, to be content" (Philippians 4:11). I say to (husband's name) this day, "The LORD bless you and keep you; the LORD make His face shine upon you, and be gracious to you; the LORD lift up His countenance upon you, and give you peace" (Numbers 6:24-26).

❧❧❧

Enter into His gates with thanksgiving, and into His courts with praise. Be thankful to Him, and bless His name.

PSALM 100:4

His Marriage

Lord, I pray You would protect our marriage from anything that would harm or destroy it. Shield it from our own selfishness and neglect, from the evil plans and desires of others, and from unhealthy or dangerous situations. May there be no thoughts of divorce or infidelity in our hearts, and none in our future. Set us free from past hurts, memories, and ties from previous relationships, and unrealistic expectations of one another. I pray that there be no jealousy in either of us, or the low self-esteem that precedes that. Protect us from influences like alcohol, drugs, gambling, pornography, lust, or obsessions. Let nothing come into our hearts and habits that would threaten our marriage in any way.

❧❧❧

Two are better than one, because they have a good reward for their labor.
For if they fall, one will lift up his companion. But woe to him who is
alone when he falls, for he has no one to help him up.

ECCLESIASTES 4:9,10

His Marriage

Lord, I pray that You would unite my husband and me in a bond of friendship, commitment, generosity, and understanding. Eliminate our immaturity, hostility, or feelings of inadequacy. Help us to make time for one another alone, to nurture and renew our marriage and remind ourselves of the reasons we were married in the first place. I pray that (husband's name) will be so committed to You, Lord, that his commitment to me will not waver, no matter what storms come. I pray that our love for each other will grow stronger every day, so that we will never leave a legacy of divorce to our children.

❦

Now to the married I command, yet not I but the Lord:
A wife is not to depart from her husband. But even if she does depart,
let her remain unmarried or be reconciled to her husband.
And a husband is not to divorce his wife.

1 CORINTHIANS 7:10,11

His Emotions

*L*ord, You have said in Your Word that You redeem our souls when we put our trust in You (Psalm 34:22). I pray that (husband's name) would have faith in You to redeem his soul from negative emotions. May he never be controlled by depression, anger, anxiety, jealousy, hopelessness, fear, or suicidal thoughts. Specifically I pray about (area of concern). Deliver him from this and all other controlling emotions (Psalm 40:17). I know that only You can deliver and heal, but use me as Your instrument of restoration. Help me not to be pulled down with him when he struggles. Enable me instead to understand and have words to say that will bring life.

❧❧❧

I waited patiently for the LORD; and He inclined to me, and heard my cry.
He also brought me up out of a horrible pit, out of the miry clay,
and set my feet upon a rock, and established my steps.
He has put a new song in my mouth—praise to our God;
many will see it and fear, and will trust in the LORD.

PSALM 40:1-3

His Emotions

Lord, I pray that You would set my husband free of negative emotions. Release him to share his deepest feelings with me and others who can help. Liberate him to cry when he needs to and not bottle his emotions inside. At the same time, give him the gift of laughter and ability to find humor in even serious situations. Teach him to take his eyes off his circumstances and trust in You, regardless of how he is feeling. Give him patience to possess his soul and the ability to take charge of it (Luke 21:19). Anoint him with "the oil of joy" (Isaiah 61:3), refresh him with Your Spirit, and set him free from any destructive emotions this day.

❧❧

He who trusts in his own heart is a fool,
but whoever walks wisely will be delivered.
PROVERBS 28:26

His Walk

O LORD, I know the way of man is not in himself; it is not in man who walks to direct his own steps" (Jeremiah 10:23). Therefore, Lord, I pray that *You* would direct my husband's steps. Lead him in *Your* light, teach him *Your* way, so he will walk in *Your* truth. I pray that he would have a deeper walk with You and an ever-progressing hunger for Your Word. May Your presence be like a delicacy he never ceases to crave. Lead him on Your path and make him quick to confess when he strays from it. Reveal to him any hidden sin that would hinder him from walking rightly before You. May he experience deep repentance when he doesn't live in obedience to Your laws.

❧❧❧

LORD, who may abide in Your tabernacle?
Who may dwell in Your holy hill?
He who walks uprightly, and works righteousness,
and speaks the truth in his heart.

PSALM 15:1,2

His Walk

*L*ord, I pray that You would create a clean heart in my husband and renew a steadfast spirit within him. Don't cast him away from Your presence, and do not take Your Holy Spirit from him (Psalm 51:10,11). Your Word says that those who are in the flesh cannot please You (Romans 8:8). So I pray that You will enable (husband's name) to walk in the Spirit and not in the flesh and thereby keep himself "from the paths of the destroyer" (Psalm 17:4). As he walks in the Spirit, may he bear the fruit of the Spirit, which is love, joy, peace, patience, kindness, goodness, faithfulness, gentleness, and self-control (Galatians 5:22,23).

❧❧❧

*H*e who walks righteously and speaks uprightly, he who despises the gain of oppressions, who gestures with his hands, refusing bribes, who stops his ears from hearing of bloodshed, and shuts his eyes from seeing evil: he will dwell on high; his place of defense will be the fortress of rocks; bread will be given him, his water will be sure.

ISAIAH 33:15,16

His Talk

*L*ord, I pray Your Holy Spirit would guard my husband's mouth so that he will speak only words that edify and bring life. Help him to not be a grumbler, complainer, a user of foul language, or one who destroys with his words, but be disciplined enough to keep his conversation godly. Your Word says a man who desires a long life must keep his tongue from evil and his lips from speaking deceit (Psalm 34:12,13). Show him how to do that. Fill him with Your love so that out of the overflow of his heart will come words that build up and not tear down. Work that in my heart as well.

❧❧❧

*Let no corrupt word proceed out of your mouth,
but what is good for necessary edification,
that it may impart grace to the hearers.*

EPHESIANS 4:29

His Talk

*L*ord, may Your Spirit of love reign in the words my husband and I speak to each other so that we don't miscommunicate or wound one another. Help us to show each other respect, speak words that encourage, share our feelings openly, and come to mutual agreements without strife. Lord, You've said in Your Word that when two agree, You are in their midst. I pray that the reverse be true as well—that You will be in our midst so that we two can agree. Let the words of our mouths and the meditations of our hearts be acceptable in Your sight, O Lord, our strength and our Redeemer (Psalm 19:14).

The words of a wise man's mouth are gracious,
but the lips of a fool shall swallow him up.

ECCLESIASTES 10:12

His Repentance

Lord, I pray that You would convict my husband of any error in his life. Let there be "nothing covered that will not be revealed, and hidden that will not be known" (Matthew 10:26). Cleanse him from any secret sins and teach him to be a person who is quick to confess when he is wrong (Psalm 19:12). Help him to recognize his mistakes. Bring him to full repentance before You. Let his suffering come from a remorseful heart and not because the crushing hand of the enemy has found an opening into his life through unconfessed sin. Lord, I know that humility must come before honor (Proverbs 15:33). Take away all pride that would cause him to deny his faults and work into his soul a humility of heart so that he will receive the honor You have for him.

❧❧❧

Search me, O God, and know my heart; try me, and know my anxieties; and see if there is any wicked way in me, and lead me in the way everlasting.

PSALM 139:23,24

His Deliverance

$\mathcal{L}$ord, You have said to call upon You in the day of trouble and You will deliver us (Psalm 50:15). I call upon You now and ask that You would work deliverance in my husband's life. Deliver him from anything that binds him. Set him free from (name a specific thing). Lift him away from the hands of the enemy (Psalm 31:15). Bring him to a place of understanding where he can recognize the work of evil and cry out to You for help. If the deliverance he prays for isn't immediate, keep him from discouragement and help him to be confident that You have begun a good work in him and will complete it (Philippians 1:6). Give him the certainty that even in his most hopeless state, when he finds it impossible to change anything, You, Lord, can change everything.

❧❧❧

$\mathcal{T}$he Lord is my rock and my fortress and my deliverer; my God, my strength, in whom I will trust; my shield and the horn of my salvation, my stronghold. I will call upon the Lord, who is worthy to be praised; so shall I be saved from my enemies.

PSALM 18:2,3

His Deliverance

Lord, help my husband to be strong in You so that he will be delivered from his enemy. Enable him to put on the whole armor of God, so he can stand against the wiles of the devil in the evil day. Help him to gird his waist with truth and put on the breastplate of righteousness, having shod his feet with the preparation of the gospel of peace. Enable him to take up the shield of faith, with which to quench all the fiery darts of the wicked one. I pray that he will take the helmet of salvation, and the sword of the Spirit, which is the Word of God, praying always with all prayer and supplication in the Spirit, being watchful and standing strong to the end (Ephesians 6:13-18).

❧❧❧

Because he has set his love upon Me, therefore I will deliver him;
I will set him on high, because he has known My name.

PSALM 91:14

His Obedience

*L*ord, You have said in Your Word that if we regard iniquity in our hearts, You will not hear (Psalm 66:18). I want You to hear my prayers, so I ask You to reveal where there is any disobedience in my life, especially with regard to my husband. Show me if I'm selfish, unloving, critical, angry, resentful, unforgiving, or bitter toward him. I confess it as sin and ask for Your forgiveness. I pray that You would also give (husband's name) a desire to live in obedience to Your laws and Your ways. Reveal and uproot anything he willingly gives place to that is not of You. Help him to bring every thought and action under Your control. Remind him to do good, speak evil of no one, and be peaceable, gentle, and humble (Titus 3:1,2).

❧❧

*M*y son, do not forget my law, but let your heart keep my commands;
for length of days and long life and peace they will add to you.
Let not mercy and truth forsake you; bind them around your neck,
write them on the tablet of your heart.

PROVERBS 3:1-3

His Obedience

*L*ord, I pray that You would give my husband a heart to obey You. Reward him according to his righteousness and according to the cleanness of his hands (Psalm 18:20). Show him Your ways, O Lord; teach him Your paths. Lead him in Your truth, for You are the God of his salvation (Psalm 25:4,5). Make him a praising person, for I know that when we worship You we gain clear understanding, our lives are transformed, and we receive power to live Your way. Help him to hear Your specific instructions to him and enable him to obey them. Give him a longing to do Your will and may he enjoy the peace that can only come from living in total obedience to Your commands.

❧✦❧

*O*bey My voice, and I will be your God, and you shall be My people.
And walk in all the ways that I have commanded you,
that it may be well with you.

Jeremiah 7:23

His Self-Image

*L*ord, I pray that (husband's name) will find his identity in You. Help him to understand his worth through Your eyes and by Your standards. May he recognize the unique qualities You've placed in him and be able to appreciate them. Enable him to see himself the way You see him, understanding that "You have made him a little lower than the angels, and You have crowned him with glory and honor. You have made him to have dominion over the works of Your hands; You have put all things under his feet" (Psalm 8:4-6). Quiet the voices that tell him otherwise and give him ears to hear Your voice telling him that it will not be his perfection that gets him through life successfully—it will be Yours.

❧❧❧

*We all, with unveiled face, beholding as in a mirror the glory of the Lord,
are being transformed into the same image from glory to glory,
just as by the Spirit of the Lord.*

2 Corinthians 3:18

His Self-Image

Lord, I pray that You would reveal to my husband that "he is the image and glory of God" (1 Corinthians 11:7), and he is "complete in Him, who is the head of all principality and power" (Colossians 2:10). Give him the peace and security of knowing that he is accepted, not rejected, by You. Free him from the self-focus and self-consciousness that can imprison his soul. Help him to see who *You* really are so he'll know who *he* really is. May his true self-image be the image of Christ stamped upon his soul. I say to you, (husband's name), "Arise, shine; for your light has come! And the glory of the LORD is risen upon you" (Isaiah 60:1).

❧❧❧

Whom He foreknew, He also predestined to be conformed to the image of His Son, that He might be the firstborn among many brethren.

ROMANS 8:29

His Faith

$\mathcal{L}$ord, I pray that You will give (husband's name) an added measure of faith today. Enlarge his ability to believe in You, Your Word, Your promises, Your ways, and Your power. Put a longing in His heart to talk with You and hear Your voice. Give him an understanding of what it means to bask in Your presence and not just ask for things. May he seek You, rely totally upon You, be led by You, put You first, and acknowledge You in everything he does. Lord, You have said in Your Word that "whatever is not from faith is sin" (Romans 14:23). May my husband be free from the sin of doubt in his life.

❧❧❧

$\mathcal{L}$et him ask in faith, with no doubting, for he who doubts is like
a wave of the sea driven and tossed by the wind.
For let not that man suppose that he will receive anything from the Lord;
he is a double-minded man, unstable in all his ways.

JAMES 1:6-8

His Faith

*L*ord, You've said that "faith comes by hearing, and hearing by the word of God" (Romans 10:17). I pray that You would feed my husband's soul with Your Word so his faith grows big enough to believe that with You all things are possible (Matthew 19:26). Give him unfailing certainty that what You've promised to do, You will do (Romans 4:21). Make his faith a shield of protection. Put it into action to move the mountains in his life. Your Word says, "The just shall live by faith" (Romans 1:17); I pray that he will live the kind of faith-filled life You've called us all to experience. May he know with complete certainty "how great is Your goodness, which You have laid up for those who fear You, which You have prepared for those who trust in You" (Psalm 31:19).

❧❦❧

*H*aving been justified by faith,
we have peace with God through our Lord Jesus Christ.

Romans 5:1

His Future

𝓛ord, I pray that You would give (husband's name) a vision for his future. Help him to understand that Your plans for him are for good and not evil—to give him a future and a hope (Jeremiah 29:11). Fill him with the knowledge of Your will in all wisdom and spiritual understanding that he may have a walk worthy of You, fully pleasing You, being fruitful in every good work and increasing in the knowledge of You (Colossians 1:9,10). May he live by the leading of the Holy Spirit and not walk in doubt and fear of what may happen. Help him to mature and grow in You daily, submitting to You all his dreams and desires, knowing that "the things which are impossible with men are possible with God" (Luke 18:27).

❧❧

𝓘 know the thoughts that I think toward you,
says the Lord, *thoughts of peace and not of evil,*
to give you a future and a hope.

Jeremiah 29:11

His Future

$\mathcal{L}$ord, I pray that (husband's name) will always conduct himself in a way that invests in his future. Keep him from losing his sense of purpose and fill him with hope for his future as an "anchor of the soul, both sure and steadfast" (Hebrews 6:19). Give him "his heart's desire" (Psalm 21:2) and keep him fresh and flourishing and bearing fruit into old age (Psalm 92:13,14). And when it comes time for him to leave this earth and go to be with You, may he have such a strong vision for his eternal future that it makes his transition smooth, painless, and accompanied by peace and joy. Until that day, I pray he will find the vision for his future in You.

❦

One thing I have desired of the LORD, that will I seek:
that I may dwell in the house of the LORD all the days of my life,
to behold the beauty of the LORD, and to inquire in His temple.

PSALM 27:4